Blogging Content
60 Great Ideas For Your Next Blog Post

Barry J McDonald

ISBN-13:
978-1491237663

ISBN-10:
149123766X

CONTENTS

INTRODUCTION

One of the worst parts of blogging is coming up with great content on a consistent basis? Even if you're the best blogger in the world, there will be days when you'll find yourself sitting in front of a blank screen wondering what today's post will be. So what can you do when no ideas seem to be flowing, well here's 60 tips to get the ball rolling and your creative juices flowing. I've included some blank space after each tip to record any thoughts or ideas that immediately spring to mind as you read them.

Great Places To Find Blog Ideas Online

Yahoo Answers http://answers.yahoo.com/ - Whether you agree or disagree with the advice given on Yahoo answers, it's a great place for finding questions that your target market are asking. So why not take a popular question or group of questions from your niche and then answer it on your blog. If some of the answers given to your chosen question are any good you can also use this in your article's research. Just be aware not to plagiarise and provide original content. (If you want to speed up the process I recommend you take a look at thisKindle Answers software here http://bit.ly/J0c8vU)

....
....
....
....
....
....

Youtube.com www.YouTube.com - With all the great free content on YouTube.com you'd be crazy not to make use of it. You can either simply embed a video on your blog or watch some videos on your given topic while taking notes. This can give you plenty of tips, tricks and advice that your readers would love to know.

....
....
....
....
....
....

Forums – One way to write content that's right up your reader's street is to hang out in forums. In forums you'll find the problems and topics that mean the most to your target audience. If you're not sure where to look for forums, a quick search on Google.com using your main keyword+forum (for example *weight loss+forum*). When you find the right forum, scroll to the most popular or active areas in the forum. This way you're guaranteed to find topics that matter most to your audience. Anything that's less active and older are probably best avoided as this is probably not as hot as it used to be.

....
....
....
....
....
....

FAQ - Are there frequently asked questions that your readers are constantly asking you or asking in forums? Why not use those questions for your next blog post. It's easy to think that just because you know all the answers, everyone else does too? Don't be mistaken there may be beginners to your topic that know very little. The best part of these types of blog post are that they're evergreen (they never grow out of date) and you can refer new readers to again and again them thus saving you time answering the same question again and again.

....
....
....
....
....
....

Google News https://news.google.com/ - Nobody likes to visit a blog whose content is outdated and not current and Google News is a great way to keep up to date with what's happening worldwide in your niche. On this great site you'll find news articles, video and other content from blogs and news sites from all over the web on almost every kind of topic you could think of. A simple search in the main search box using your main keyword, will reveal numerous articles with all the latest news and tips. For ease of use you can also subscribe to their email updates and get the latest news straight to your emails inbox every time your keyword is triggered.

....
....

....
....
....
....

Google Search Bar – Where would we be without Google? Love them or hate them they can get a mine of great ideas for blog posts. One way is to use the Google search bar for ideas. Take your main keyword and add a space + a (for example - weight loss a), you'll soon see Google trying to complete the search term for you. If you can't find what you want, do the same but add a space plus the letter "b". By going through the alphabet you'll find unlimited article titles and ideas to write about.

....
....
....
....
....
....

Amazon.com www.Amazon.com - Amazon is a treasure trove of great research and content ideas for your blog. Firstly, find the bestselling books on your topic then use the "Look Inside" feature to scroll through the books contents. Each topic/section/chapter title is some area where the author feels the reader needs to know about. "Bingo" you've got a selection of great blog post ideas.

....
....
....
....
....
....

Magazines www.magazines.com - Again like Amazon.com, publishers of magazines need to research their audience well or they'd never make any money. Pick a magazine related to your industry and check out the magazine covers. The most prominent news stories are always on the front cover. If the magazine owner feel that these are the most important topics to write about, maybe you should also.

....
....
....
....
....
....

Blog Comments – Has there been any blog comments that would make a great blog post? A question, a statement a reader made, or did you commenter feel you could have added more on this topic? Even if you've only got a new blog that hasn't got any comments yet, you can always visit a competitor's blog and use one of their blogs comments. Then when you're finished your blog post, write a comment on their blog and link back to your blog post. It's both an easy way to get free traffic and more content for your blog.

....
....
....
....
....
....

PLR "Private Label Rights" - Private label rights products which can be in the form of articles, ebooks, software, etc., which you can sell with your name as the owner and author to. It's a great way to build products and create content quickly, leaving you more free time to do things that you love doing. If you choose to go this route, you've got 2 options you can either use the PLR content as is OR you use the bones of the article as an idea generator for blog posts of your own. To find PLR for your market, just type you can use PLR+YourKeyword into Google.com for places where you can purchase your material. One place I recommend and where I purchase PLR articles is www.EasyPLR.com

....

....
....
....
....
....

Hire A Ghost Writer - Although PLR is a handy way to generate content quickly, the same content does end up on different blogs and sites all over the internet. If you'd like content that's solely yours and can't be read anywhere else, you could hire a ghost writer for your next blog post. When looking for ghost-writers try Elance.com or some of the other reputable writing sites on the internet. It may cost you more money, but it will free up that writing time so you can spend it elsewhere on your business.

....
....
....
....
....
....

Ezinearticles.com – www.Ezinearticles.com is one of the largest content sites on the internet where you'll find articles on every subject you could ever think of. You can use this site 2 ways, you can either use an article off the site free of charge as long as follow the terms of use OR do a quick search for the most popular articles on your niche. This is a great way to find what your readers have shown an interest in and it's probably what you should be writing about.

....
....
....
....
....
....

Sales Letters - Are there any products related to your blogs topic? If there are, why not take some time to read the sales copy. In all sales letters you'll find areas that the copywriter feels are important to his or her customers. If the copywriter feels them important enough to include in his sales letter it's probably wise that your readers will want to know about them also. To find products related to your niche, type your keyword into Google.com BUT instead of looking at the normal search results take a look at the AdWords ads down the right hand side of the page. Most of these ads are bought by people trying to sell their products and services. Another place to find products for sale is www.Clickbank.com a quick search on their marketplace may provide something related to your niche where you can use their sales letters for reference.

....
....
....
....
....
....

Product Reviews - Following on from the previous tip is there a product you've bought lately in your niche that you've loved or hated? Why not write an honest review of the pros and cons of your purchase? If it's a good product your readers will probably want to know about it and if it's NOT, your readers will definitely want to know about it. When reviewing products always give your honest opinion as your readers will appreciate you more for it. Also if the product has an affiliate program (you get paid for a portion of the sale) sign up, and get paid for promoting the product in your blog post.

....
....
....
....
....
....

Twitter www.Twitter.com - Is there a trending topic on Twitter.com that's relevant to your blogs subject? Why not write about it and discuss it on your blog. You can also take a discussion that's been happening on your Facebook page and bring it over to your blog. This is a great way to not only write great content but also to make people aware of your Twitter and

Facebook accounts and get new followers.

....
....
....
....
....
....

Get In A Blog Mastermind – Why not team up with other bloggers for advice and tips. You could met up on Facebook or Twitter and brainstorm ideas, like how to get blog post ideas, ways to promote blog posts, etc. No successful blogger ever made it on their own and you won't be the exception. Asking for help and providing help to others will help you to build a long and successful blogging career.

....
....
....
....
....
....

Spoof Post - Although this can really only be used on April 1st, you could write a spoof post that gives some type of shocking news that people may actually fall for. Plus if you write it well and its half way believable it could go viral and send lots of free traffic your way.

....
....
....
....
....
....

Ask Your Readers – Always give your readers what they're looking for but if you're not sure just ask. By asking your readers for content ideas you're 100% guaranteed to give your readers exactly what they're looking for.

....
....

....
....
....
....

Read Other Blogs – Reading a variety of other blogs outside your niche can be a great way to stimulate your mind with content ideas. You should never copy other peoples content straight out but could you could take their blog title or content and put your own personal spin on it?

....
....
....
....
....
....

Update Old Content - Time has moved on and maybe it's time to go back through your archives to update your content? Are there any techniques or tips that aren't useful anymore? Are there posts you could make stronger by adding more tips, a video, or new resource to. Don't think that having a blog means your content is set in stone. By being up to date and conscious of providing great content you'll attract new readers, like bee's to honey.

....
....
....
....
....
....

Resource Posts - Are there any posts on your blog that go well together? Go back through your archives and pull all those posts together into one post. Then just write a brief introduction to each post and a hyperlink to each of the full articles. This a great way to get readers to spend more time on your blog by getting them to go deeper into your content.

....
....

. . . .
. . . .
. . . .
. . . .

Blog Statistics - Do you know what your most popular posts are? If you've got a self-hosted WordPress blog it's easy to find a wordpress plugin that can do this for you. If haven't got a WordPress blog (you really need one) a quick look into your web hosting statistics will reveal what pages get the most traffic. This is probably the posts that your audience likes best, so why not serve up more of the same.

. . . .
. . . .
. . . .
. . . .
. . . .
. . . .

Other Peoples Content - Read an article, blog or seen a video lately that you totally agreed or disagreed with? Was it something that made you think? Or something that you could have added some tips to? Why not talk about it in your next blog post. If you find that the latter is the most relevant, why not write your tips and then tell the blog owner about your post. If they're really into providing quality content to their readers they may promote your post on their blog and send some free traffic and new readers your way.

. . . .
. . . .
. . . .
. . . .
. . . .
. . . .

Guest Blog – If things are really dire, why not take a break from your blog and do a spot of guest blogging on other blogs. It will take your mind off your blog and the pressure of coming up with content for yourself. Plus guest blogging is a great way to show your talents to a new audience and build your own blogs following. Then when your creative juices are flowing again, head back and start pumping out more great content.

Review A Blog – Is there a blog on your topic that you love to read, a place that provides great content to its readers, then why not promote in on your blog? Do a simple here's why you need to visit this blog and give a link to it. You might think that doing this will work against you and rob you of traffic but you'd be wrong it's a great way to share great content with your readers.

....
....
....
....
....
....

Email – Have you received any email with catchy titles or content that made you think that would be a wonderful post title or idea? Although you might think you need to read other great blogs to write a great blog post, there are blog post ideas everywhere.

....
....
....
....
....
....

Great Places To Find Blog Ideas Offline

C.o.n.t.e.n.t - This a big content favourite of Jimmy D Brown. Basically take a word from your industry and write your blog post around it. For example I wrote a post on "Motivation" on my blog. In it I took each letter separately and wrote a point about each. (M - Momentum - I wrote a point on momentum and how it refers to motivation O – Observe – then I wrote a point about how to observe your progress for motivation purposes) and so on with the rest of the letters of the word "MOTIVATION", you get the idea. It's a simple idea but one that you can come back to again and again.

....
....
....
....
....
....

Blockuster Movie - Is there a quote or a part from the latest blockbuster film that you could use to emphasize a point from your industry. Randy Gage from www.RandyGage.com has used this in the past to show how some of the latest blockbuster movies are filled with lack programming when it comes to prosperity consciousness.

....
....
....
....
....
....

Friends And Family - Is your niche related to something that we all use or know about? If so, why not quiz family and friends for blog ideas. Is there something your friends would like to know about your niche topic or problems they had with your niche topic? Chances are, if they've got questions they need answered, your blog readers will as well.

....

....
....
....
....
....

Upcoming Events - Are there any upcoming events, seminars, etc coming up in your business that you feel your readers should know about. Is there a speaker coming to your area? By giving your readers more than just simple blog posts you become the "go to guy or gal" when it comes to advice and news on your given topic.

....
....
....
....
....
....

Life - Has something happened in your life that's relevant to your topic? Is there a lesson you've learned that you feel could help hammer home a point you're constantly making to your readers? Even if it's not exactly on the topic, could you turn this experience into a learning or entertaining piece for your readers.

....
....
....
....
....
....

Hero Worship - Is there someone in your industry known or unknown that you'd like to give recognition to? Someone that's helped you or made a difference in your business or life? Why not write a blog post about them? If this person has products or services that have helped you, why not send your readers there also. And like a previous tip if there's an affiliate scheme you could make some money at the same time. BUT only do this if you are genuinely grateful to this person and not as a sneaky way to make money off your readers, which defeats the whole purpose.

....
....
....
....
....
....

Mistakes - What's the biggest mistake you've made or others have made working in your niche? Nobody like making mistakes and if there's a lesson in it why not give it to your readers. They'll appreciate the advice and you'll come across as being more human and not being beyond making mistakes.

....
....
....
....
....
....

Gift Ideas - Would your blog readers be interested in gift ideas for people in your niche? If you write about "Dogs" could you write an article on gifts for dog owners? Or gift ideas for scrap book makers or gift ideas for fitness fanatics? If you're not sure how to put one of these articles together, let www.Amazon.com do the research for you. Search for the top 5 - 10 products being sold in your niche, these are products your blog audience may be really interested in. Now write a simple countdown blog post (10 to 1) with a small summary of each product and a link to the Amazon store (your affiliate link of course)

....
....
....
....
....
....

Save Money - The way things are nowadays nobody wants to have to spend more money than they have to. So why not make a post full of money saving tips? If there ways to purchase products cheaply that are not well known? Is there a site that's offering money off coupons? Highlight them in your blog post and watch the traffic come flooding in.

....
....
....
....
....
....

Apps - Are there any apps that would be useful to your audience? For example are your readers into running? Would a running app help them to train better? Although you might know all the coolest apps out there in the market place, don't assume everyone else does.

....
....
....
....
....
....

Holidays - Could you write a blog post closely related St Patrick, Valentines, or Christmas day? If no known publics holidays are coming up why not highlight an obscure one that your reader's people mightn't know about, and then write a new blog post about it.

....
....
....
....
....
....

Interview An Expert – Is there someone in your industry that you admire and look up to, then why not ask for an interview? You don't have to take up much of their time, a simple request questions could be "Could you possibly answer this question for me? or "Have you got 5 tips that have really helped you?" All experts were beginners at one stage and if they're worth their salt they'll gladly help you out. To get in touch with your expert most are available through Twitter, Facebook or at their blog. If they've haven't the time to help out, don't take it badly ask if they have any articles or previous interviews that you could use instead.

....
....
....
....
....
....

Key People In Your Business – Who are the key people in your business? If I was a beginner to your area of expertise, who are the people that I should look out for? Who creates the best products that could really help me, what other blogs should I be reading? Like I wrote previously make content with beginners in mind, who knows they may turn into long time readers?

....
....
....
....
....
....

A – Z of Topics – Like the content idea earlier on in this book, why not take a letter from the "Alphabet" and use it for a topic idea. If I was writing on weight loss the letter "A" would be for "Aerobics" and I'd write a post on aerobics. Then "B" could be for weight loss "Buddy" and how to use a weight loss buddy to help you lose weight (you get the idea). If everything works perfectly you'd have 26 posts, why not challenge yourself and see if you can do it?

....
....
....
....

....
....

This Day In History – Hands up who loves history? When not go
back in time and write a period piece, how has your industry changed
in the last year or even further back, 10 years ago? What beliefs did
people in your niche think was true that now are completely wrong?
What has been proven to come true?

....
....
....
....
....
....

What Would You Change – What do you hate the most about your
industry? Or if you had a magic wand what would you change about
your industry? Nothings perfect, so why not show up the
imperfections and who knows you might get a change happening.

....
....
....
....
....
....

Your Industry In Your Country/State – Does your business differ
from state to state or country to country? Should your readers know
of laws, rules and conditions as they apply to each area. Can they sell
real estate without a licence here but not over in the next the state or
vice versa? What should they look out for when buying product "A"
in the U.S but not in Europe? If there are differences be sure to tell
your readers don't assume they already know. They'll be grateful for
the advice.

....
....
....
....
....

....

Predictions For The Future – Where do you see your niche going to in the next 12 months, 5 years or 10 years? Is there a breakthrough happening that's going to put everything on its head? Or do you personally have a prediction of where you'd like your industry to go? This is a great blog post idea that works great as the last post of the year but if you've got a great idea why wait and use it today.

....

....

....

....

....

....

Definitions Of Your Business – Are there definitions or terms that are unique to your business and not in the real world? For example, do you use finance terms that the ordinary person wouldn't know about, or slang words for surfing positions? Not everyone coming to your blog will be an expert on these so why not write a post on commonly used terms and break them down into plain English.

....

....

....

....

....

....

Get Away From Your Computer – Ever have total writers block sitting in front of the computer and then suddenly get a great idea in the shower or when out for a walk. Staring at a blank computer screen can be the worst place for coming up with your next blog post idea. Take a break, go for a walk, read a book do anything that'll take your mind off blogging and don't be surprised that the ideas coming flooding to you.

....

....

....

....

....
....

Write An Opposite Post – Ever written a post on the positive side on something but also knew that you could have written one just as good on the negative side? For example – 5 Reasons To Home School For Kids" could also become "5 Reasons Why You Should Never Home School Your Kids" Why not become devil's advocate and see what you could come with?

....
....
....
....
....
....

Write It Down - Never ever, leave home without a pen and paper because chances are your next blog post idea going to happen far from the PC. There an old saying "The best way to pin down an idea is with a pen". So always keep a pen and paper on hand for when those "Eureka" ideas come to mind.

....
....
....
....
....
....

Weekly Round Up – Why not make Friday a weekly round up day? Gather all this weeks post, news, gossip etc, into one simple blog post. While we all would love readers who return on a daily basis, it doesn't happen. So why not make up a simple weekly digest of what happening to keep them up to speed.

....
....
....
....
....
....

Stir Up Controversy - Being controversial can be a great way to grab lots of free publicity for your blog. But get it wrong and you could go down in flames. Try to find ways to be controversial but not nasty for the sake of being nasty. If you genuinely have a reason for taking this person of topic to hand back it up with reasons of why it's so. Not everyone will agree with you but some new readers will admire you for not being afraid of putting your head on the chopping block.

....
....
....
....
....
....

Tip List – Everyone loves tips, if fact that's why you bought this book. Why not make a list of the top 10 things to do, 5 sites to visit, 7 things to say, 9 places to avoid, etc. This gives your readers something they'll love to read full of pure content without the added filler.

....
....
....
....
....
....

Do A Survey – If you've got a large number of readers why not survey them? It's a great way to come up with ideas for posts, products to sell, and ways to improve your blog. Firstly ask a question that you'd like to know from your readers, Do they purchase books on "your topic" or what's the most amount of money they've made online? It's important that your question makes both the reader comfortable answering and also makes them want to know how everyone else answered the question? This way when you do a follow up post on the survey results, you'll get more readers coming back for the answers.

....
....
....

....
....
....

Use Stumbleupon Or I'm Feeling Lucky – Why not do your own Alice in Wonderland impression and tumble down the strange, weird and wacky paths of the internet. Just put your main keyword into Google.com and hit the "I'm feeling lucky option and see where you end up? Or visit StumbleUpon.com, use your main keyword and find out what weird and wonderful sites come up. Yes, it may be a toss of the dice where you end up, but you may come across tons of great ideas for your next upcoming posts.

....
....
....
....
....
....

Post A Humorous Picture Or Story – Is there a humorous picture or story online that's related to your blogs topic. Blogs should be entertaining as well as informative, if you've been informative for a long period why not throw a bit of humour into the mix.

....
....
....
....
....
....

"Should And Should Not!" Posts – What are "the should" or "should not's" in your industry or topic? For example could you write about things you should never say at an interview, or why you should never spank your child or why you should always make sure you buy holiday insurance?" This can be an easily to create a killer post that can stand the test of time and never go out of date.

....
....
....

....
....
....

What Would "Blank Celebrity" Do In Your Situation? – I've used this tip personally for a blog post on weight loss, the title read - "What could Simon Cowell could teach you about weight loss! In it I pointed out how Simon Cowell is always honest with his opinion and are you as a dieter honest with yourself. Just take the characteristics of your chosen celebrity and mould your blog post around them.

....
....
....
....
....
....

Read More – Maybe you've drained the creative well dry and it's time to give it a rest. Take a few days off blogging and do some reading about your subject. Reading is great for not only giving your more creative ideas but it will also help make you a better writer. Keep the old motto in mind "Leaders Are Readers".

....
....
....
....
....
....

Give Yourself The Day Off – Finding and creating great content is half the battle in blogging but who said you have to do it on your own. Make it known to other blogs in your niche that you're always looking for great content and would they be interested in doing a guest post on your blog. If they agree give it a go and if it all works out well you could both swap places for a week and write content for each other's blog?

....
....
....
....

. . . .
. . . .

Short And Sweet – Are you expecting too much of yourself providing content. Do you feel you really need to write a 900 word article every day for your blog? If so ease back on how much you provide and see if your readers notice the difference. You may be surprised that they come back more often for your daily tid-bits rather than having to read "War And Peace" on a daily basis!

. . . .
. . . .
. . . .
. . . .
. . . .
. . . .

And finally (whew!!!) - Do you have more text articles than video on your blog? Why not go back through your old archives and bring it back in the form of video. Not everyone out there is a big lover of text so why not cater to this audience with videos instead? If the thoughts of going in front of a camera is daunting make a simple video using slides with text and pictures. But why not take the leap and give video a go, it's a great way for readers to see the person behind the blog.

. . . .
. . . .
. . . .
. . . .
. . . .
. . . .

Recommended Reading

While I may have provided great content in this book I'd be amiss not to recommend other great books out there that can take your blogging to the next level.

How To Make Money Blogging: How I Replaced My Day-Job With My Blog by Bob Lotich

http://www.amazon.com/How-Make-Money-Blogging-ebook/dp/B0091ISTUU

31 Days to Finding Your Blogging Mojo by Bryan Allain

http://www.amazon.com/Days-Finding-Your-Blogging-ebook/dp/B005MGUFX4

ProBlogger: Secrets for Blogging Your Way to a Six-Figure Income by Darren Rowse and Chris Garrett

http://www.amazon.com/ProBlogger-Secrets-Blogging-Six-Figure-ebook/dp/B0077FDAC6

www.ingramcontent.com/pod-product-compliance
Lightning Source LLC
LaVergne TN
LVHW052126070326
832902LV00038B/3972